When the Wind Blows

Kim Hutchens

Presentation by *BookLeaf Publishing*

Web: www.bookleafpub.com

E-mail: info@bookleafpub.com

ISBN: 9789357740395

First edition 2023

Kelsey, Hunter, Cody, Sophie, and Brent -
You will always be my reason.

ACKNOWLEDGEMENT

For I am convinced that neither death nor life, neither angels nor demons, neither the present nor the future, nor any powers, neither height nor depth, nor anything else in all creation, will be able to separate us from the love of God that is in Christ Jesus our Lord. -Romans 8:38-39

My Favorite

You were my favorite
Except when you called too much
You were my favorite
Except when you would overthink
You were my favorite
Except when your bad mood spilled out

You were my favorite
When you gave hugs freely
You were my favorite
When you remembered every occasion
You were my favorite
When you created amazing moments

You were my favorite
Except when you needed too much
You were my favorite
Except when you got sick
You were my favorite
Except when you left without a goodbye

You were my favorite
When your laugh filled the room
You were my favorite
When you stay in every memory
You were my favorite
You were my favorite.

Love

Some see love in money
Some in time
Others in a feeling
Or an instant
Some see it in the past
Some in possessions
Others in their work

I think love is in the peace
Of giving my soul to you
While you do the same
An exchange
A sacrifice to hold you
More important than myself.

Every Day Words

You don't really know someone
Unless you know their struggles
Just knowing a name is not knowing
It's shallow to think so

Only knowing does not make a family
Family means great sacrifice
That springs forward
Because of the love
You carry

How haphazard to use false words
To manipulate others
Into feeling they owe a debt
To work

Work barely knows and never
Sacrifices
Beyond its own convenience
Always wanting more of you for its own greed
Don't be fooled.

A Sunday Nap

In my sleep you once whispered
Over and over how you loved me
As you gently moved the hair
Away from my brow,
And you meant it.
It was your secret,
But I hold it.
And I still remember
That in that one space and time
I was truly loved,
And you meant it.

Failure

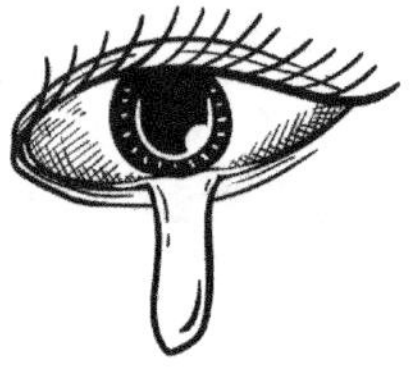

I memorized your words
Not intentionally
But I hear them
In the darkest times.
They are not uplifting
Nor sit with good intent.
They were meant to tear down,
And they did,
And they do.
It is
The gift you left.

An Idea

In the silence a word comes
And hangs just above my reach
Floating down at its own pace
With a chest full of despair
Then an idea is born

Grace is Bigger

Grace is bigger
Than the box I put it in
Grace is bigger than how I think
Or how I feel
Grace is bigger than what I give
It flows with second chances
That I would hold back
Grace is bigger than the sea
A mystery bigger than me
For it is best I don't fully understand
Or it would be something to take
Something to break
But it must be given not stolen
Grace is too big to put in a pocket
It spills over all who ask

The Chair

A Christmas present
The first together purchase
A place of complete peace
Laughter lives in that chair
Famous episodes in that chair
Always communication there
How could two fit?

Two fit comfortably
A place for new music
Questions in that chair
Spirits intertwined in that chair
Always renewal there
How could two fit?

Years pass and the music ends
Space between replaces peace
Silence happens in that chair
Goodbyes said in that chair
Always clarity there
Chairs are meant for one

Where Does Happiness Go?

Where does happiness go
When it's not with me
Does it sit in a church pew
Or hover over an empty alter
Perhaps it floats down on the dogwood limb
Or lands softly as dew on cut grass

Could it rest in a dissonant cord
Resonate in perfect family harmony
Sit in a pile of graded papers
Or behind a finished project
Maybe it lingers in the smell of fresh paint
Or on the easel

Perhaps it lands in a show stopping number
Sleeping in a created moment that begs
    repeating
Or lands in the sunlight sliding through a storm
    cloud
Maybe it waits in the footprints hiding on the
    wooded path
Perhaps it lies in the blanket on the sofa
Or in an unwrapped gift under the tree

Where does happiness go
When it's not with me
Maybe it lives with the memories
Where it grows and grows
While finding safety
From those who crush it with a word

Perhaps it lifts with the wind
That flows through an open car window.
Maybe it lives on the dirt road where the
    blackberries grow
And rides in the bed of the brown pickup truck
Or explodes in the laughter of my children
Reminding me that it will find me again
In due time

The Reel

My mind won't turn off
That conversation
Our children
Laundry
Unfinished work on my desk
The sliding glass door to the past
Old performances
Too many games
Did he understand?
Unpacking crates
Cleaning that wall
Making her bedroom
An unpaid bill
Only 30 minutes
Reset the alarm
The lines the lines the lines

My mind won't turn off
Another conversation
The children
Red eyes
Goodbyes
Futures
A line for writing
Find a black truck
Words always unsaid
Beautiful places
Picking blackberries
What will be remembered?
Only 30 minutes
Reset the alarm
The lyric the lyric the lyric

This Time

I give you my days
But you keep your own
My sacrifice is great
You have many gains
It's too hard
It's easy
There's no end
I don't remember the beginning
Starting over sounds good
Then sounds like exhaustion
Sweet melodies of music
Cover it all
The wheel starts again
Maybe it will be different
This time

Love Note

Did you leave me a note
Surely I missed it
Where you tell me how sorry
You are for all the ways
You let me slip away

I missed it somehow
But it has to be somewhere
Cause I'm sure you felt sorry
For all the pain living in your place
And the years that can never erase

It must be hidden somewhere
A treasure to find in an empty drawer
With all the baggage and doubt
That you left in your wake
Where's the note for heaven's sake?

The Mess

I often wonder
About the mess when I'm gone.
I'm not the cleanest;
Creativity takes space.
When you throw away my trinkets,
You will never know why I held
On to them so tightly.
You will make your summations,
Your thoughtful insight,
But you'll really never know.
You will clean, curse, and ponder
Life
And then move on.

And in your older angst
Your search for more time
More meaning
You will have a faint memory.
When you choose to create
Or clean
A trinket, a memory
That you thought you forgot.
Oh yes, and think what will they do
With the mess when you're gone.
Then remember me
And take the secret with you.

When It's Time

Life gives you things to say
When you struggle to find your voice
Or to say it the way others can hear
I know that now.

I Forgot to Tell You

I don't tell you enough
You make me bold
You know my ways
I don't tell you
But the thoughts are there.

I don't tell you enough
That love runs like roots
Woven into the important parts
I don't tell you
But the thoughts are there.

I don't tell you enough
That you rescued me
And what we built is good
I don't tell you
But the thoughts are there.
The thoughts are always there.

Truth Survives

There's nothing left to say
When silent strength sits in truth
A cold death to your crooked path
Snow blankets the footprints left
Like salt in a wound.

There's nothing left to say
The limb has lost its last leaf
And the sunlight will sneak through
While new seeds bring future hopes
The buds won't bloom in gray.

Let the rain continue to wash
The lies that still prevail
And kill the low growing weeds
Give an ax to the ivy
With a final blow.

There is nothing left to say
When silent strength sits in truth.
The wind will still howl
In a new season
But for a different flower.

For the Daughters

The girls are in the house
One mind
One passion
Beauty with driven spirits
Stubbornness to achieve more
Tenderness beyond the past.

The girls are in the house
One thought
One dream
Committed beyond limited minds
Empathy for those who went before
Determination without fear of failure.

The girls are in the house
One heart
One purpose
Fearless as distractions dance
Forgiving while accepting imperfections
Creating new ways.

The Last Time

I touched your back
You turned and looked me in the eye
I didn't know it was the last time.

You asked me not to go.
I pretended I had no feelings.
I didn't know it was the last time.

You asked if I loved you.
I said no.
I didn't know it was the last time.

Remember

Be the light
Give more than you take
Elaborate your ideas
Find the good
Show the love of Jesus
And be the light.

It's never too late
Dreams don't expire
Good comes with bad
Dig deep and hold fast
And be the light.

Add the wow
Write a letter
Breathe in the moment
Listen before you speak
And be the light.

Be willing to be still
Read the Word
Spend time with creation
Extend grace
And be the light.

Perspective

It's all in perspective
What you have
Or what you don't
What's a burden
Or a gift
Who you'll love
And who you won't

It's all in perspective
An opportunity
Or a block
What's a win
Or a loss
Who is poor
And who is not.

A Gift

My words aren't fancy
Like polished pearls
But they're mine
And I give them to you.

My love's not showy
Like a spring bouquet
But it's true
And I'll share it with you.

My song's not angelic
Like a symphony
But it's honest
And I'll sing it for you.